BUTTERBALL®

MAKES IT EASY!

Butterball® Makes It Easy!	2
Cooking Fast	6
Cooking Lean	20
Cooking For Two	34
Cooking For A Family	46
Cooking Retro	62
Make It & Take It	74
Cooking For A Crowd	82
Product Index	92
Recipe Index	94

BUTTERBALL®
MAKES IT EASY!

Whether you're a struggling novice or a seasoned gourmet, when it comes to cooking, **BUTTERBALL® MAKES IT EASY!** This book features a full complement of great-tasting, nutritious recipe ideas using Butterball Turkey and Chicken products. They are the perfect alternatives for virtually every eating occasion year-round.

The Best of All is Butterball™! And if you're like millions of Americans, when you think turkey you think Butterball! It's America's favorite turkey! For more than 40 years, Butterball has been the brand name known and trusted for consistently tender and juicy premium quality turkey.

But turkey is no longer *just* for Thanksgiving. As consumer eating habits and lifestyles have changed, Butterball has responded by adding more and more products. Today, the Butterball brand name is featured on the widest selection of fresh and frozen turkey and chicken products on the market.

This collection of recipes demonstrates how **BUTTERBALL® MAKES IT EASY** when "Cooking Fast," "Cooking Lean," "Cooking For Two," "Cooking For A Family," "Cooking Retro," "Make It & Take It" and "Cooking For A Crowd." Each recipe provides the complete preparation time, that is, the preparation time and cooking time from start to finish, along with nutritional information. Try one today!

If you would like more Butterball product information, visit our year-round site on the Internet at http://www.butterball.com. And during November through December, for questions about turkey preparation, call the Butterball Turkey Talk-Line™ toll free at 1-800-323-4848, or for the hearing impaired 1-800-TDD-3848.

Traditional, Fresh and Frozen Whole and Li'l Butterball® Turkey

These turkeys make the perfect centerpiece for holiday gatherings and year-round special occasions. And, they cook up great on the grill in the summer.

Butterball® Fresh and Frozen Bone-In Breast, Boneless Turkey and Boneless Breast

The ideal turkey choices for breast meat lovers when planning small get-togethers, or to supplement a whole turkey for larger feasts.

Butterball® Fully Cooked Whole Turkey

These convenient, *fully cooked* turkeys are ready to serve in a fraction of the time of a regular turkey. Just heat and serve or slice cold. Choose from three delicious taste varieties: Baked, Honey Roasted and Smoked.

Butterball® Frozen Stuffed Turkey

Stuffed with traditional herb bread stuffing, this turkey goes from freezer to oven with no thawing.

Butterball® Holiday Turkey Dinner

Ultimate Convenience...Each fully prepared holiday dinner includes: a fully cooked Butterball® Baked Turkey, Butterball® Turkey Gravy, Butterball® Herb Seasoned Stuffing, mashed potatoes and cran-applesauce. Contact your local grocery store's meat or deli counters for availability.

Butterball® Fresh Premium Turkey

For everyday meal convenience, these fresh turkey products offer various tender and juicy cuts that are recipe ready. They are surprisingly easy to prepare and a delicious way to freshen up your weekly menu.

- FRESH BONELESS SKINLESS TURKEY BREAST PRODUCTS (Turkey Breast Cutlets, Turkey Breast Roast, Turkey Breast Medallions, Turkey Breast Strips, Turkey Breast Tenderloins, Ground Turkey Breast)

- FRESH BONELESS TURKEY PRODUCTS (Ground Turkey, Turkey Burger Patties, Turkey Hot Italian Sausage, Turkey Sweet Italian Sausage, Turkey Breakfast Sausage Links)

Butterball® Fresh Chicken Products

A complete line of fresh, USDA Grade A chicken products, all specially trimmed and selected to be low in fat, extra tender, juicy and delicious. Look in your grocer's fresh meat section.

- FRESH BONELESS SKINLESS CHICKEN PRODUCTS (Breast Fillets, Thin Breast Fillets, Breast Tenders, Thigh Cutlets)

- FRESH SEASONED BREAST FILLETS (Teriyaki, Italian, Mesquite, Lemon Butter)

- FRESH BONE-IN CHICKEN (Best of the Fryer, Split Breasts, Drumsticks, Thighs, Wings, Skinless Split Breasts, Skinless Thighs)

- FRESH WHOLE CHICKEN (Young Roaster)

Butterball® Chicken Requests™

Quick & Easy From The Freezer! A tasty line of tangy, zesty, spicy and crispy baked chicken breasts that are lightly breaded in five delicious flavors: Original, Italian Herb, Lemon Pepper, Parmesan and Southwestern. They are *BAKED, NOT FRIED* and ready to serve in just minutes after heating. Look for them in your grocer's freezer section.

Butterball® Ready-To-Eat Turkey Products

These great-tasting, nutritious alternatives for traditional lunch, weeknight dinner and breakfast meat favorites, are all made from premium quality Butterball® Turkey. Choose from a selection of products in different flavors to satisfy all of your taste needs.

- FAT FREE & REGULAR TURKEY LUNCH MEATS
- DELI THIN SLICED TURKEY MEATS
- FAT FREE & REGULAR TURKEY FRANKS

- FAT FREE & REGULAR SLICE 'N SERVE™ BREAST OF TURKEY (Oven Roasted, Honey Roasted, Hickory Smoked, Mesquite Smoked, Barbecue, Rotisserie Seasoned)

- FAT FREE & REGULAR TURKEY SMOKED SAUSAGE
- TURKEY BACON
- HEAT & SERVE TURKEY BREAKFAST SAUSAGE LINKS & PATTIES

Butterball® Deli Poultry Products

A wide variety of consistently high quality deli poultry products that are freshly sliced at your grocer's deli counter. Each product is *oven rack roasted* and guaranteed to taste tender and delicious every time.

- OVEN ROASTED BREASTS (Turkey, Less Sodium Chicken)
- SPECIALTY TURKEY BREASTS (Browned, Honey Roasted and Smoked, Smoked, Mesquite Smoked)
- FLAVORED TURKEY BREASTS (Cajun Style, Peppered, Lemon Pepper, Italian Style, Southwest Salsa)
- LUNCH MEATS (Turkey Pastrami, Turkey Ham, Turkey Salami, Turkey Bologna)

We're sure you'll agree... *BUTTERBALL® MAKES IT EASY because The Best of All is Butterball™!*

Please Note: Not all Butterball Turkey and Chicken products are available in all areas.

COOKING
FAST

Voila! Captivating creations in 25 minutes or less! When time is of the essence, choose from Quickest Chicken Cacciatore, sassy Grilled Jalapeño Turkey Burgers or Turkey Tostadas piled high with juicy turkey strips, avocado and garden-fresh tomatoes. Cooking has never been easier.

Grilled Jalapeño Turkey Burgers

- **1 package (1¼ pounds) Butterball® Lean Fresh Ground Turkey**
- **¼ cup chopped green onions**
- **2 tablespoons chopped pickled jalapeño peppers or mild green chilies**
- **1 clove garlic, minced**
- **1 teaspoon Worcestershire sauce**
- **½ teaspoon salt**
- **⅛ teaspoon black pepper**

Prepare grill for medium-direct-heat cooking. Lightly spray unheated grill rack with nonstick cooking spray. Combine all ingredients in large bowl; mix well. Form into six large patties. Grill 6 minutes on each side or until meat is no longer pink in center. Serve with your favorite condiments.

Makes 6 burgers

● Preparation Time: 15 minutes ●

Nutritional Information per Burger:
Calories: 80, Fat: ½g, % of Calories from Fat: 6, Sodium: 360mg

Chicken Caesar Salad

1 package Butterball® Chicken Breast Tenders
¼ cup prepared Caesar salad dressing
½ teaspoon minced garlic
6 cups torn romaine lettuce
1 large tomato, cut into wedges
1½ cups Caesar-flavored croutons
½ cup shredded Parmesan cheese
Anchovy fillets, optional

Combine chicken, salad dressing and garlic in large skillet. Cook over medium-high heat 4 to 5 minutes or until no longer pink in center, turning frequently to brown evenly. Divide romaine lettuce among 4 plates. Top with tomato and croutons. Arrange chicken tenders on top of each salad. Sprinkle with Parmesan cheese; top with anchovy fillets. Serve with additional salad dressing.

Serves 4

● Preparation Time: 15 minutes ●

Nutritional Information per Serving:
Calories: 230, Fat: 12g, % of Calories from Fat: 48, Sodium: 530mg

TIP
Call us at 1-800-BUTTERBALL year-round
or check our web page at
http://www.butterball.com. To reach the
Butterball® Turkey Talk-Line in November and
December call 1-800-323-4848.

Chicken Caesar Salad

Oriental Dinner Salad

1 Butterball® Chicken Requests™ Original Crispy Baked Breast
3 cups torn mixed salad greens (spinach, romaine and
    mesclun mix)
1 orange, peeled and cut into sections
2 tablespoons sliced green onion
½ cup chow mein noodles
1 teaspoon sesame seeds

Oriental Vinaigrette:
  2 tablespoons vegetable oil
  2 teaspoons reduced sodium soy sauce
  ½ teaspoon sesame oil, optional
  ¼ teaspoon grated fresh ginger

Prepare chicken according to package directions. Whisk together
vinaigrette ingredients. To assemble salad, place orange and
onion on mixed greens. Top with sliced chicken; drizzle with
vinaigrette. Sprinkle with chow mein noodles and sesame
seeds.

Serves 1

● Preparation Time: 20 minutes ●

Nutritional Information per Serving:
Calories: 650, Fat: 41g, % of Calories from Fat: 57, Sodium: 960mg

Antipasto Dinner Salad

1 Butterball® Chicken Requests™ Italian Style Herb Crispy
    Baked Breast
3 cups torn mixed salad greens (romaine, radicchio and
    iceberg lettuce)
1 tablespoon sun-dried tomatoes in oil, drained and chopped
1 ounce light mozzarella cheese, sliced
1 tablespoon pine nuts or almonds
¼ cup grated fresh Parmesan cheese, optional

Italian Vinaigrette:
  2 tablespoons olive oil
  1 tablespoon prepared pesto
  1 teaspoon balsamic vinegar or red wine vinegar

Prepare chicken according to package directions. Whisk together vinaigrette ingredients. To assemble salad, place tomatoes and mozzarella cheese on mixed greens. Top with sliced chicken; drizzle with vinaigrette. Sprinkle with nuts and Parmesan cheese.

Serves 1

● Preparation Time: 20 minutes ●

Nutritional Information per Serving:
Calories: 680, Fat: 46g, % of Calories from Fat: 60, Sodium: 2100mg

Butterball® Sweet Italian Sausage with Vesuvio Potatoes

1 package Butterball® Lean Fresh Turkey Sweet Italian Sausage
4 baking potatoes, cut lengthwise into wedges
2 tablespoons olive oil
½ teaspoon coarse ground black pepper
1 can (14½ ounces) chicken broth
6 cloves garlic, minced
½ cup dry white wine
6 tablespoons minced fresh parsley
2 tablespoons shredded Parmesan cheese
Salt

Grill sausage according to package directions. Combine potatoes, oil and pepper in large bowl. Spray large nonstick skillet with nonstick cooking spray; add potato mixture. Cook 15 minutes. Add chicken broth and garlic; cook, covered, 10 minutes or until potatoes are tender. Add wine and parsley; cook, uncovered, 5 minutes. Sprinkle with Parmesan cheese. Add salt to taste. Serve with grilled sausage.

Serves 6

● Preparation Time: 30 minutes ●

Nutritional Information per Serving:
Calories: 260, Fat: 13g, % of Calories from Fat: 46, Sodium: 830mg

Turkey on Focaccia Rolls

2 packages (6 ounces each) Butterball® Fat Free Oven Roasted
   Deli Thin Sliced Turkey Breast
½ cup mayonnaise
3 tablespoons Dijon mustard
2 tablespoons crumbled blue cheese, optional
6 (4-inch) focaccia rolls, cut in half, toasted
6 tomato slices
6 Swiss cheese slices
2 avocados, peeled and sliced
2 cups finely shredded romaine lettuce

Combine mayonnaise, mustard and blue cheese in medium bowl. Spread mayonnaise mixture on each bottom half of roll. Layer turkey, tomato, Swiss cheese, avocado and lettuce onto rolls. Cover with top halves of rolls; cut in half.

Makes 12 half sandwiches

● Preparation Time: 20 minutes ●

Nutritional Information per Serving:
Calories: 370, Fat: 18g, % of Calories from Fat: 43, Sodium: 790mg

TIP
*Butterball® Turkey Deli products
are naturally lean—several varieties
are 100% fat free and are available in many
delicious flavors.*

Turkey on Focaccia Roll

Turkey Tostadas

1 package Butterball® Fresh Boneless Turkey Breast Strips
1 tablespoon vegetable oil
1 tablespoon chili powder
½ teaspoon salt
8 (6-inch) tostadas or corn tortillas
1 cup fat free vegetarian refried beans
2 cups shredded iceberg lettuce
1 cup (4 ounces) shredded low fat Cheddar cheese
1 avocado, coarsely chopped
1 cup chopped tomato
½ cup chopped green onions

Heat oil in large nonstick skillet over medium heat until hot. Add turkey strips; sprinkle with chili powder and salt. Cook and stir frequently about 5 minutes or until no longer pink. Spread each tostada with 2 tablespoons refried beans. Divide shredded lettuce evenly among tostadas. Place cooked turkey strips on top of lettuce; sprinkle with cheese. Add avocado, tomato and onions to each tostada. Serve with low fat sour cream and salsa, if desired.   *Makes 8 tostadas*

● Preparation Time: 20 minutes ●

Nutritional Information per Tostada:
Calories: 430, Fat: 23g, % of Calories from Fat: 49, Sodium: 630mg

TIP
*To assure safe, tender,
juicy fresh cuts, cook turkey until
no longer pink in center being
careful not to overcook.*

Turkey Tostada

Quickest Chicken Cacciatore

4 Butterball® Boneless Skinless Chicken Thighs
2 tablespoons butter or margarine
1 jar (14 ounces) chunky-style meatless spaghetti sauce
1 jar (2½ ounces) sliced mushrooms, drained
½ cup chopped green bell pepper
¼ cup dry red wine
**1 package (9 ounces) refrigerated fettuccine, cooked and
  drained**

Cut each thigh lengthwise into 3 pieces. Melt butter in large
skillet over medium heat. Add chicken; cook 8 to 10 minutes or
until no longer pink in center. Add remaining ingredients except
fettuccine. Cook and stir until heated through. Serve over
fettuccine.   *Serves 4*

● Preparation Time: 15 minutes ●

Nutritional Information per Serving:
Calories: 360, Fat: 16g, % of Calories from Fat: 42, Sodium: 660mg

Turkey Apple Grill

**1 Butterball® Fully Cooked Smoked Young Turkey, thawed,
  sliced thin**
4 tablespoons butter or margarine
8 slices marbled rye bread
⅓ cup sour cream
⅓ cup chutney
1 tart apple, cored and sliced thin
1 cup (4 ounces) shredded Swiss cheese

Butter one side of each slice of bread. Turn buttered side down. Combine sour cream and chutney. Spread 2 tablespoons sour cream mixture on each slice of bread. Top half of the slices with turkey, apple and cheese. Top with remaining bread slices, buttered side up. Heat large skillet or griddle over medium heat until hot. Cook sandwiches about 3 minutes on each side or until golden brown and heated through.   *Makes 4 sandwiches*

● Preparation Time: 15 minutes ●

Nutritional Information per Sandwich:
Calories: 590, Fat: 32g, % of Calories from Fat: 47, Sodium: 1040mg

Turkey Tortilla Soup

1 package (1¼ pounds) Butterball® Lean Fresh Ground Turkey
1 teaspoon olive oil
2 cans (14½ ounces each) 100% fat free reduced sodium chicken broth
1 jar (16 ounces) mild or medium-hot salsa
1 can (11 ounces) Mexican-style corn, drained
1 tablespoon fresh lime juice
2 to 3 tablespoons chopped fresh cilantro
2 ounces baked tortilla chips
Salt and black pepper
Lime wedges

Heat oil in large saucepan over medium heat until hot. Brown turkey in saucepan 6 to 8 minutes or until no longer pink, stirring to separate meat. Add chicken broth, salsa, corn and lime juice to saucepan. Reduce heat to low; simmer, covered, about 10 minutes. Ladle into bowls. Sprinkle with cilantro. Add salt and pepper to taste. Serve with tortilla chips and wedge of lime.   *Serves 8*

● Preparation Time: 25 minutes ●

Note: To make your own tortilla strips, cut flour tortillas into thin strips and bake in 400°F oven until crisp. Serve on top of soup.

Nutritional Information per Serving:
Calories: 190, Fat: 6g, % of Calories from Fat: 26, Sodium: 890mg

"LET'S TALK TURKEY" FROM THE DELI ...

*To make your own Deluxe Deli Sandwiches at home, stock
your refrigerator with a few flavor favorites then
"mix and match" in creative combinations. Use contrasts
of flavors and textures to add interest—and remember, we eat with
our eyes first, so stack the sandwich high and make it colorful.
To make **Butterball**® Deluxe Deli Sandwiches try...*

Thin Sliced from the Deli

Butterball® Peppered Turkey Breast
Butterball® Oven Roasted Turkey Breast
Butterball® Honey Roasted Turkey Breast
Butterball® Smoked Turkey Breast

On Interesting Breads

Pita
Focaccia
Tortillas
Sun-dried Tomato Bread
Croissants
3-Grain Bread
Nut Bread

Topped with Crisp or Crunchy

Sliced Tart Apple
Shredded Cucumber
Green and Yellow Bell Pepper Rings
Vinaigrette Slaw
Pepperoncini
Radish Sprouts

With Signature Spreads

Bacon and Blue Cheese Mayonnaise
Chutney and Honey Mustard
Cranberry Butter
Yogurt and Fresh Herbs
Salsa and Refried Beans
Green Onions and Hummus
Caesar Mayonnaise

*Assorted Deluxe
Deli Sandwiches*

COOKING LEAN

Spice up your dinner repertoire with nutritious and delicious Turkey with Fiery Thai Sauce, Zydeco Chicken or Caribbean Grilled Turkey. With such full-flavored hearty dishes, eating lean no longer means leaving the table hungry.

Thai Stir Fry

1 package Butterball® Chicken Breast Tenders
1 tablespoon oil
½ cup red and yellow bell pepper strips
1 clove garlic, minced
1 tablespoon chopped fresh cilantro
1 teaspoon grated fresh ginger
2 tablespoons reduced sodium soy sauce
1 teaspoon brown sugar

Heat oil in large skillet over medium heat until hot. Cook and stir chicken about 6 minutes on each side or until golden brown. Add bell peppers, garlic, cilantro, ginger, soy sauce and brown sugar to skillet. Reduce heat to low; cover and simmer 4 minutes longer. Serve over rice or lo mein noodles, if desired.

Serves 4

● Preparation Time: 15 minutes ●

Nutritional Information per Serving:
Calories: 100, Fat: 3½g, % of Calories from Fat: 30, Sodium: 550mg

Turkey Cutlets with Chipotle Pepper Mole

1 package Butterball® Fresh Boneless Turkey Breast Cutlets
1 can (14½ ounces) chicken broth
¼ cup raisins
4 cloves garlic, minced
1 chipotle chile pepper in adobo sauce
2 tablespoons ground almonds
2 teaspoons unsweetened cocoa
½ cup chopped fresh cilantro
2 tablespoons fresh lime juice
½ teaspoon salt

To prepare chipotle sauce, combine chicken broth, raisins, garlic, chile pepper, almonds and cocoa in medium saucepan. Simmer over low heat 10 minutes. Pour into food processor or blender; process until smooth. Add cilantro, lime juice and salt. Grill cutlets according to package directions. Serve chipotle sauce over grilled cutlets with Mexican polenta.*   *Serves 7*

*To make Mexican polenta, cook 1 cup instant cornmeal polenta according to package directions. Stir in ½ teaspoon garlic powder, ½ teaspoon salt and 2 cups taco-seasoned cheese.

● Preparation Time: 20 minutes ●

Nutritional Information per Serving:
Calories: 130, Fat: 2g, % of Calories from Fat: 15, Sodium: 580mg

Turkey Cutlet with
Chipotle Pepper Mole

Matchstick Stir Fry

1 package Butterball® Fresh Boneless Turkey Breast Strips
1 tablespoon cornstarch
1 cup orange juice
1 tablespoon reduced sodium soy sauce
1 clove garlic, minced
2 teaspoons grated orange peel
2 teaspoons minced fresh ginger
1 teaspoon sugar
½ teaspoon salt
¼ teaspoon red pepper flakes
1 tablespoon vegetable oil
¼ pound snow peas, trimmed
2 small carrots, cut into thin strips
1 small onion, cut into strips
1 small red bell pepper, cut into thin strips
2 oranges, peeled and sectioned

Combine cornstarch, orange juice, soy sauce, garlic, orange peel, ginger, sugar, salt and red pepper flakes in small bowl. Stir until mixture is smooth; set aside. Heat oil in large skillet or wok over high heat until hot; add turkey. Cook and stir 4 to 5 minutes or until turkey is no longer pink; remove from skillet. Add snow peas, carrots, onion and bell pepper. Cook and stir 1 minute; remove from skillet. Add cornstarch mixture to skillet. Cook and stir until mixture thickens; add turkey and vegetables. Reduce heat to low; simmer, covered, 1 minute. Add orange sections. Serve with almond rice, if desired.   *Serves 6*

● Preparation Time: 20 minutes ●

Note: If short on time, substitute packaged frozen stir fry blend vegetables for fresh vegetables.

Nutritional Information per Serving:
Calories: 180, Fat: 3g, % of Calories from Fat: 17, Sodium: 330mg

Jalapeño Grilled Chicken with Baja Pasta

2 packages Butterball® Chicken Split Breasts
¼ cup jalapeño jelly
2 tablespoons fresh lime juice

Combine jalapeño jelly and lime juice in small saucepan. Heat over medium heat, stirring constantly, until melted and smooth. Grill chicken breasts 15 to 20 minutes on each side or until internal temperature reaches 170°F and no longer pink in center. Brush jalapeño mixture on chicken during last 10 minutes of grilling. Serve with Baja Pasta. *Serves 6*

Baja Pasta

½ pound angel hair pasta, broken
1 can (14½ ounces) fat free reduced sodium chicken broth
1 can (14½ ounces) mild diced tomatoes for chili
¼ cup sliced green onions
2 tablespoons chopped fresh cilantro

Toast angel hair pasta in large nonstick skillet over medium heat until lightly browned. Stir in chicken broth, tomatoes and onions. Simmer 5 minutes or until pasta is tender. Stir in cilantro.

● Preparation Time: 30 to 40 minutes ●

Nutritional Information per Serving:
Calories: 330, Fat: 2½g, % of Calories from Fat: 6, Sodium: 380mg

Grilled Chicken Breasts with Tropical Salsa

1 package Butterball® Skinless Boneless Chicken Breast Fillets
1 cup cubed mango
1 kiwi, diced
2 green onions, chopped
2 tablespoons chopped fresh cilantro
1 tablespoon fresh lime juice
½ teaspoon red pepper flakes

Grill chicken fillets 4 to 5 minutes on each side or until internal temperature reaches 170°F and no longer pink in center. Combine mango, kiwi, onions, cilantro, lime juice and red pepper flakes in medium bowl. Serve with chicken.   *Serves 4*

● Preparation Time: 20 minutes ●

Nutritional Information per Serving:
Calories: 150, Fat: ½g, % of Calories from Fat: 3, Sodium: 250mg

Turkey with Fiery Thai Sauce

1 (3-pound) Butterball® Boneless Breast of Young Turkey with Gravy Packet, thawed
½ red bell pepper, sliced thin
1½ cups water
2 tablespoons reduced sodium soy sauce
1 teaspoon red curry paste
1 tablespoon chopped fresh cilantro

Roast turkey according to package directions. Combine gravy packet, bell pepper, water, soy sauce and curry paste in medium saucepan. Simmer over medium heat 10 minutes. Stir in cilantro. Serve with turkey breast and lo mein noodles, if desired.   *Serves 8*

● Preparation Time: 10 minutes plus roasting time ●

Nutritional Information per Serving:
Calories: 170, Fat: 8g, % of Calories from Fat: 41, Sodium: 250mg

Grilled Chicken Breast with Tropical Salsa

Louisiana Zydeco Chicken

 4 Butterball® Boneless Skinless Chicken Breast Fillets
1½ teaspoons paprika
 1 teaspoon cayenne pepper
 1 teaspoon black pepper
 ½ teaspoon garlic powder
 ½ teaspoon chili powder
 ½ teaspoon salt
 1 tablespoon olive oil

Combine paprika, cayenne pepper, black pepper, garlic powder, chili powder and salt in small bowl. Coat chicken breasts with spice mixture. Heat oil in medium skillet over medium heat until hot. Add chicken; cook 4 to 5 minutes on each side or until no longer pink in center. Excellent served with red beans and rice.

Serves 4

● Preparation Time: 15 minutes ●

Nutritional Information per Serving:
Calories: 150, Fat: 4g, % of Calories from Fat: 23, Sodium: 520mg

Hearty Turkey Soup

 8 ounces Butterball® Fat Free Turkey Smoked Sausage, cut
    into chunks
 8 ounces fresh mushrooms, quartered
 ½ large onion, chunked
 2 medium carrots, sliced
 3 large cloves garlic, minced
 3 medium red potatoes, cubed
 1 can (14½ ounces) diced tomatoes with roasted garlic
 1 can (14½ ounces) low salt, 98% fat free chicken broth
 ¼ cup quick-cook barley
 1 can (15 ounces) small white beans
 ¼ cup chopped fresh Italian parsley
    Salt and black pepper
    Grated Parmesan cheese

Spray large heavy saucepan with nonstick cooking spray. Add mushrooms, onion, carrots and garlic; cook over medium heat, stirring constantly, about 5 minutes. Add potatoes, tomatoes, chicken broth and barley. Cover; simmer about 10 minutes. Stir in undrained beans, sausage and parsley. Simmer 5 minutes. Add salt and pepper to taste. Serve with grated Parmesan cheese.

Serves 8

● Preparation Time: 30 to 40 minutes ●

Nutritional Information per Serving:
Calories: 360, Fat: 2½g, % of Calories from Fat: 5, Sodium: 1580mg

Turkey with Hoisin Sauce and Oriental Vegetables

1 (3-pound) Butterball® Boneless Young Turkey with Gravy Packet, thawed
1 cup sliced shiitake mushrooms
2 cloves garlic, minced
1 tablespoon minced fresh ginger
2 teaspoons vegetable oil
1½ cups water
1 tablespoon hoisin sauce

Roast boneless turkey according to package directions. Combine mushrooms, garlic, ginger and oil in medium saucepan. Cook and stir over medium heat 5 minutes. Stir in contents of gravy packet, water and hoisin sauce. Reduce heat to low; simmer 5 to 10 minutes. Serve turkey and hoisin sauce over cooked oriental vegetables, if desired.

Serves 8

● Preparation Time: 10 minutes plus roasting time ●

Nutritional Information per Serving:
Calories: 180, Fat: 10g, % of Calories from Fat: 50, Sodium: 730mg

Moroccan Grilled Turkey with Cucumber Yogurt Sauce

1 package Butterball® Fresh Boneless Turkey Breast Cutlets
⅓ cup fresh lime juice
2 cloves garlic, minced
½ teaspoon curry powder
½ teaspoon salt
¼ teaspoon ground cumin
¼ teaspoon cayenne pepper
3 large pitas, cut in half*

Prepare grill for medium-direct-heat cooking. Lightly spray unheated grill rack with nonstick cooking spray. Combine lime juice, garlic, curry powder, salt, cumin and cayenne pepper in medium bowl. Dip cutlets in lime juice mixture. Place cutlets on rack over medium-hot grill. Grill 5 to 7 minutes on each side or until meat is no longer pink in center. Place turkey and Cucumber Yogurt Sauce in pitas.   *Serves 6*

*Pitas may be filled and folded in half.

Cucumber Yogurt Sauce

1 cup fat free yogurt
½ cup shredded cucumber
1 teaspoon grated lime peel
1 teaspoon salt
½ teaspoon ground cumin

Combine yogurt, cucumber, lime peel, salt and cumin in medium bowl. Chill.

● Preparation Time: 20 minutes ●

Nutritional Information per Serving:
Calories: 170, Fat: 0g, % of Calories from fat: 0, Sodium: 800mg

Moroccan Grilled Turkey with
Cucumber Yogurt Sauce

Caribbean Grilled Turkey

1 package Butterball® Fresh Boneless Turkey Breast
  Tenderloins
4 green onions
4 cloves garlic
2 tablespoons peach preserves
2 tablespoons fresh lime juice
1 teaspoon salt
1 teaspoon shredded lime peel
1 teaspoon bottled hot sauce
1 teaspoon soy sauce
¼ teaspoon black pepper

Lightly spray unheated grill rack with nonstick cooking spray.
Prepare grill for medium-direct-heat cooking. In food processor
or blender, process onions, garlic, preserves, lime juice, salt,
lime peel, hot sauce, soy sauce and pepper until smooth. Spread
over tenderloins. Place tenderloins on rack over medium-hot
grill. Grill 20 minutes or until meat is no longer pink, turning
frequently for even browning.   *Serves 6*

● Preparation Time: 25 minutes ●

Nutritional Information per Serving:
Calories: 100, Fat: ½g, % of Calories from Fat: 5, Sodium: 450mg

Turkey Stuffed Chiles Rellenos

1 package (1½ pounds) Butterball® 99% Fat Free Fresh Ground
  Turkey Breast
1 envelope (1¼ ounces) taco seasoning mix
⅓ cup water
6 large poblano chilies, stems on, slit lengthwise and seeded
1 cup (4 ounces) shredded reduced fat Cheddar cheese
1½ cups tomato salsa

Spray large nonstick skillet with nonstick cooking spray; heat over medium heat until hot. Brown turkey in skillet over medium-high heat 6 to 8 minutes or until no longer pink, stirring to separate meat. Add taco seasoning and water. Bring to a boil. Reduce heat to low; simmer 5 minutes, stirring occasionally. In separate pan, cook chilies in boiling water 5 minutes; remove and drain. Combine turkey mixture and Cheddar cheese. Fill chilies with mixture. Pour salsa into 11×7-inch baking dish. Place stuffed chilies slit side up in baking dish. Bake, uncovered, in preheated 400°F oven 15 minutes. Serve hot with additional salsa and sour cream, if desired. *Serves 6*

● Preparation Time: 30 minutes ●

Nutritional Information per Serving:
Calories: 210, Fat: 4½g, % of Calories from Fat: 19, Sodium: 1000mg

Chicken Marsala

4 Butterball® Boneless Skinless Chicken Breast Fillets
3 cups sliced fresh mushrooms
2 tablespoons sliced green onion
2 tablespoons water
¼ teaspoon salt
¼ cup dry Marsala wine
1 teaspoon cornstarch

Flatten chicken fillets between two pieces of plastic wrap. Spray nonstick skillet with nonstick cooking spray; heat over medium heat until hot. Add chicken; cook 2 to 3 minutes on each side or until no longer pink in center. Transfer to platter; keep warm. Add mushrooms, onion, water and salt to skillet. Cook 3 minutes or until most of the liquid has evaporated. Combine wine and cornstarch in small bowl; add to skillet. Heat, stirring constantly, until thickened. Spoon over warm chicken. *Serves 4*

● Preparation Time: 15 to 20 minutes ●

Nutritional Information per Serving:
Calories: 140, Fat: ½g, % of Calories from Fat: 4, Sodium: 390mg

Make every day special for you and a friend with taste-tempting recipes developed to serve two with no leftovers!

Crispy Italian Herb Chicken with Tri-Color Rotini Pasta

2 Butterball® Chicken Requests™ Italian Style Herb Crispy
   Baked Breasts
1 cup uncooked tri-color rotini pasta
3 tablespoons water
1 tablespoon olive oil
2 cups broccoli florets
3 plum tomatoes, quartered
1 clove garlic, minced
   Grated Parmesan cheese

Prepare chicken according to package directions. Cook and drain pasta. Add water, oil and broccoli to skillet; cover. Cook 2 to 4 minutes. Stir in pasta, tomatoes and garlic; continue cooking 2 minutes longer. Serve chicken breasts with pasta. Sprinkle with Parmesan cheese.   *Serves 2*

● Preparation Time: 20 minutes ●

Nutritional Information per Serving:
Calories: 480, Fat: 14g, % of Calories from Fat: 27, Sodium: 650mg

Crispy Lemon Pepper Chicken with Spinach Pasta

2 Butterball® Chicken Requests™ Lemon Pepper Crispy Baked Breasts
2 cups uncooked bow tie pasta
3 tablespoons water
1 tablespoon olive oil
6 cups fresh spinach
2 cloves garlic, minced
½ cup part skim ricotta cheese
Grated Parmesan cheese, optional

Prepare chicken according to package directions. Cook and drain pasta. Add water and oil to skillet. Add spinach; cover. Cook 2 to 4 minutes or until spinach is wilted. Stir in garlic and cooked pasta; continue cooking 2 minutes longer. Add ricotta cheese; stir to blend. Serve spinach pasta topped with sliced chicken breasts. Sprinkle with Parmesan cheese.   *Serves 2*

● Preparation Time: 20 minutes ●

Nutritional Information per Serving:
Calories: 650, Fat: 20g, % of Calories from Fat: 28, Sodium: 590mg

TIP

*Chicken Requests™ Crispy Baked Breasts
are available in 5 flavors: Original,
Italian Style Herb, Parmesan,
Southwestern and
Lemon Pepper.*

**Crispy Lemon Pepper Chicken with
Spinach Pasta**

Crispy Southwestern Seasoned Chicken with Pasta Fideo

2 Butterball® Chicken Requests™ Southwestern Style Crispy
  Baked Breasts
1 tablespoon olive oil
1 cup uncooked broken angel hair pasta
¼ cup chopped green onions
1½ cups water
1 cup frozen corn
½ cup salsa
1 tablespoon chopped fresh cilantro

Prepare chicken according to package directions. Add oil to
skillet. Cook and stir pasta and onions in skillet 2 to 3 minutes or
until pasta is lightly toasted. Stir in water and corn; simmer 3
minutes. Add salsa and cilantro. Serve chicken breasts with
pasta. *Serves 2*

● Preparation Time: 20 minutes ●

Nutritional Information per Serving:
Calories: 520, Fat: 14g, % of Calories from Fat: 25, Sodium: 910mg

Ranch-Style Chicken and Pasta

2 Butterball® Boneless Skinless Chicken Breasts
½ cup prepared ranch salad dressing, divided
1 cup uncooked rotini pasta
2 cups broccoli florets
¼ cup diced red bell pepper
2 tablespoons chopped green onion

Combine chicken breasts and ¼ cup ranch salad dressing in large bowl; marinate in refrigerator 15 minutes. Cook pasta 8 minutes; add broccoli during last 3 minutes of cooking. Drain pasta and broccoli; set aside. Remove chicken from marinade; discard marinade. Grill chicken 4 to 5 minutes on each side or until no longer pink in center. Combine cooked pasta, broccoli, bell pepper and onion in large bowl. Toss with remaining ¼ cup ranch salad dressing. Serve chicken breasts with ranch-style pasta.   *Serves 2*

● Preparation Time: 30 minutes ●

Nutritional Information per Serving:
Calories: 660, Fat: 34g, % of Calories from Fat: 47, Sodium: 840mg

Pesto Pasta Turkey Toss

1 cup diced Butterball® Fat Free Slice 'N Serve Oven Roasted Breast of Turkey
1 cup small shell pasta, cooked and drained
1 tomato, cubed
¼ cup sliced green onions
¼ cup chopped roasted red peppers
2 tablespoons mayonnaise
2 tablespoons prepared pesto
2 cups torn romaine lettuce

Combine all ingredients except romaine lettuce in medium bowl. Toss to blend; chill. To serve, spoon salad over lettuce and garnish with additional roasted peppers.   *Serves 2*

● Preparation Time: 25 minutes ●

Nutritional Information per Serving:
Calories: 230, Fat: 6g, % of Calories from Fat: 22, Sodium: 690mg

Nutty-Crusted Turkey Cutlets

2 Butterball® Fresh Boneless Turkey Breast Cutlets
4 tablespoons ground walnuts
2 tablespoons grated Parmesan cheese
½ teaspoon dried Italian seasoning*
½ teaspoon salt
¼ teaspoon paprika
1 tablespoon butter or margarine
½ lemon

Combine nuts, cheese, Italian seasoning, salt and paprika in medium bowl. Generously coat both sides of each cutlet with nut mixture. Melt butter in large nonstick skillet over medium heat. Cook turkey cutlets 2 to 2½ minutes on each side or until no longer pink in center. Squeeze fresh lemon juice over cutlets.

Serves 2

*To make your own Italian seasoning blend, combine ¼ teaspoon dried oregano, ⅛ teaspoon dried basil and ⅛ teaspoon dried thyme in small bowl.

● Preparation Time: 15 minutes ●

Nutritional Information per Serving:
Calories: 250, Fat: 17g, % of Calories from Fat: 60, Sodium: 820mg

TIP
For quick lean meals, buy a package of Butterball® Fresh Premium Boneless Ground Turkey, Turkey Breast Cutlets, Medallions, Tenderloins or Strips.

Nutty-Crusted Turkey Cutlets

Pasta and Spinach with Sun-Dried Tomatoes

⅓ pound Butterball® Oven Roasted Deli Turkey Breast, sliced
    thin and cut into strips
¼ cup sun-dried tomatoes, packed in oil, drained and chopped,
    reserve oil
1 clove garlic, minced
5 ounces fresh spinach, rinsed
2 ounces bow tie pasta, cooked and drained
¼ cup Italian salad dressing
3 tablespoons feta cheese, divided

Pour 1 teaspoon reserved sun-dried tomato oil in nonstick skillet. Add turkey, tomatoes and garlic. Cook and stir over medium heat 2 minutes. Add spinach, pasta, dressing and 2 tablespoons cheese; toss to coat. Cover; warm over low heat for about 1 minute. Sprinkle with remaining 1 tablespoon cheese.

Serves 2

● Preparation Time: 20 minutes ●

Nutritional Information per Serving:
Calories: 360, Fat: 19g, % of Calories from Fat: 50, Sodium: 970mg

Turkey Tenderloin with Mushroom Sauce

1 package Butterball® Fresh Boneless Turkey Breast
    Tenderloins, use 1 tenderloin, cut into ½-inch-thick slices
1 tablespoon butter or margarine
4 ounces fresh mushrooms, sliced
½ small onion, minced
1 cup chicken broth, divided
1 tablespoon cornstarch
1½ teaspoons tomato paste
1 tablespoon chopped parsley
    Salt and black pepper

Melt butter in large nonstick skillet over medium heat. Brown tenderloin slices in skillet about 5 minutes, turning frequently. Add mushrooms and onion; cook 3 minutes. Add ½ cup chicken broth; cover and simmer about 5 minutes. Combine cornstarch, remaining ½ cup chicken broth and tomato paste; pour into skillet; stir to blend. Cook and stir until thickened. Stir in parsley. Add salt and pepper to taste.   *Serves 2*

● Preparation Time: 25 minutes ●

Nutritional Information per Serving:
Calories: 240, Fat: 8g, % of Calories from Fat: 29, Sodium: 900mg

Crispy Chicken with Mushroom Fusilli Pasta

2 Butterball® Chicken Requests™ Original Crispy Baked
   Breasts
1 cup uncooked tomato basil fusilli pasta
2 tablespoons butter or margarine
8 ounces fresh mushrooms, sliced
½ cup thin sliced onion
½ cup roasted red peppers, cut into strips
2 tablespoons chopped fresh parsley

Prepare chicken according to package directions. Cook and drain pasta. Melt butter in large nonstick skillet over medium heat. Add mushrooms and onion; cook and stir 4 minutes. Add roasted peppers and pasta; heat 2 minutes. Stir in parsley. Serve chicken breasts with pasta.   *Serves 2*

● Preparation Time: 20 minutes ●

Nutritional Information per Serving:
Calories: 540, Fat: 19g, % of Calories from Fat: 31, Sodium: 680mg

Crispy Parmesan Chicken with Penne Pasta Primavera

2 Butterball® Chicken Requests™ Parmesan Crispy Baked Breasts
1 cup uncooked penne pasta
3 tablespoons water
1 tablespoon olive oil
1 cup quartered and chunked zucchini
1 cup quartered and chunked yellow squash
½ cup thinly sliced onion, separated into rings
1 clove garlic, minced
1 tablespoon fresh basil
2 tablespoons grated Parmesan cheese, divided
Salt and black pepper

Prepare chicken according to package directions. Cook and drain pasta. Add water, oil, zucchini, squash and onion to skillet; cook and stir 2 minutes. Stir in garlic and pasta; continue cooking 2 minutes longer. Add basil and 1 tablespoon Parmesan cheese. Serve chicken breasts with pasta. Sprinkle with remaining 1 tablespoon Parmesan cheese. Add salt and pepper to taste.

Serves 2

● Preparation Time: 20 minutes ●

Nutritional Information per Serving:
Calories: 500, Fat: 16g, % of Calories from Fat: 30, Sodium: 120mg

Crispy Parmesan Chicken with
Penne Pasta Primavera

Cooking For A Family

Savor the exciting flavors of South of the Border Turkey Kabobs, juicy Hidden Herb Grilled Turkey Breast or Smoked Turkey with Summer Cranberry Nectar. These recipes will be family favorites.

South of the Border Turkey Kabobs

1 package Butterball® Fresh Boneless Turkey Breast
  Medallions
¼ cup vegetable oil
¼ cup fresh lime juice
2 teaspoons salt
1 teaspoon chili powder
½ teaspoon garlic powder
2 medium yellow squash, cut into ¾-inch chunks
2 medium onions, cut into ¾-inch chunks
2 red bell peppers, cut into ¾-inch chunks
2 green bell peppers, cut into ¾-inch chunks

Combine oil, lime juice, salt, chili powder and garlic powder in large bowl. Toss vegetables in oil mixture; stir to coat. Transfer vegetables to separate large bowl. Add turkey medallions to oil mixture; stir to coat. Thread turkey and vegetables alternately onto skewers, leaving a small space between pieces. Grill over hot coals about 20 minutes or until turkey is no longer pink in center, turning occasionally to prevent burning.   *Serves 6*

● Preparation Time: 30 minutes ●

Nutritional Information per Serving:
Calories: 190, Fat: 10g, % of Calories from Fat: 47, Sodium: 760mg

Chicago Fire Italian Sausage Sandwiches

1 package Butterball® Lean Fresh Turkey Hot Italian Sausage
5 large hot dog buns
5 teaspoons yellow mustard
5 tablespoons chopped onion
5 tablespoons pickle relish
10 tomato wedges
10 hot sport peppers

Grill sausage according to package directions. Place in buns. Add mustard, onion, relish, tomato wedges and peppers to each sandwich. *Makes 5 sandwiches*

● Preparation Time: 15 minutes ●

Nutritional Information per Sandwich:
Calories: 330, Fat: 11g, % of Calories from Fat: 30, Sodium: 2730mg

Smoked Turkey with Summer Cranberry Nectar

1 Butterball® Fully Cooked Smoked Young Turkey, thawed, sliced thin
1 can (16 ounces) whole berry cranberry sauce
  Juice of ½ lime
1 tablespoon seeded and chopped jalapeño pepper
½ teaspoon salt

Combine cranberry sauce, lime juice, jalapeño pepper and salt in food processor; process until smooth. Spoon cranberry nectar over sliced turkey. Excellent served with cranberry-studded mini-corn muffins. *Serves 6*

● Preparation Time: 15 minutes ●

Nutritional Information per Serving (3 ounces cooked turkey):
Calories: 270, Fat: 9g, % of Calories from Fat: 30, Sodium: 520mg

Chicago Fire Italian Sausage Sandwiches

Chicken Seville

4 Butterball® Boneless Skinless Chicken Breast Fillets
1 tablespoon vegetable oil
1 can (14½ ounces) diced tomatoes with roasted garlic
1 medium onion, sliced
¼ cup chicken broth
¼ cup salad olives, drained
2 cloves garlic, minced
1 teaspoon dried thyme leaves
   Salt and black pepper

Heat oil in large skillet over medium heat until hot. Brown chicken in skillet, turning to brown both sides. Add tomatoes, onion, chicken broth, olives, garlic and thyme; cover. Cook 8 to 10 minutes or until chicken is no longer pink in center. Add salt and pepper to taste. This dish is delicious served with saffron rice.

Serves 4

● Preparation Time: 15 to 20 minutes ●

Nutritional Information per Serving:
Calories: 450, Fat: 6g, % of Calories from Fat: 11, Sodium: 970mg

Turkey Cutlets with Tex-Mex Salsa

1 package Butterball® Fresh Boneless Turkey Breast Cutlets
1 can (15 ounces) black beans, rinsed and drained
1 can (11 ounces) Mexican-style corn, drained
1 cup salsa
2 tablespoons chopped fresh cilantro
1 tablespoon Mexican seasoning blend*
1 teaspoon salt
1 tablespoon vegetable oil
   Lime wedges, optional

Combine black beans, corn, salsa and cilantro in large bowl; stir to blend. Chill until served. Combine seasoning blend and salt. Dip cutlets into seasoning mixture. Heat oil in large skillet over medium heat until hot. Cook cutlets 2 to 2½ minutes on each side until lightly browned and no longer pink. Place bean salsa on serving platter; arrange cutlets on top of salsa. Serve with a squeeze of fresh lime.   *Serves 7*

*To make your own Mexican seasoning, combine 1½ teaspoons chili powder, ¾ teaspoon oregano and ¾ teaspoon cumin.

● Preparation Time: 30 minutes ●

Nutritional Information per Serving:
Calories: 160, Fat: 1g, % of Calories from Fat: 6, Sodium: 870mg

Mustard Herb Crusted Turkey Tenderloins

1 package Butterball® Fresh Boneless Turkey Breast Tenderloins
1 cup fresh bread crumbs
2 tablespoons olive oil
2 tablespoons minced fresh parsley
1 clove garlic, minced
2 teaspoons Dijon mustard
½ teaspoon dried savory leaves
½ teaspoon salt

Preheat oven to 400°F. Mix bread crumbs, oil, parsley, garlic, mustard, savory and salt in small bowl to form a coarse paste. Spread crumb mixture over tenderloins. Place in small roasting pan sprayed with nonstick cooking spray. Roast 30 minutes or until no longer pink in center.   *Serves 4*

● Preparation Time: 10 minutes plus roasting time ●

Nutritional Information per Serving:
Calories: 260, Fat: 6g, % of Calories from Fat: 19, Sodium: 580mg

Grilled Turkey with Roasted Garlic Grilled Corn

1 (4½- to 9-pound) Li'l Butterball® Young Turkey, thawed,
  giblets removed
  Vegetable oil
8 ears fresh corn in husks
1 whole bulb fresh garlic
  Olive oil

Prepare charcoal covered grill for indirect-heat cooking. Position foil drip pan in middle of bottom rack, place 25 to 30 briquettes along the outside of each lengthwise side of the drip pan. Burn briquettes until covered with gray ash, about 30 minutes. Place top rack in grill with handle openings over coals.

Turn wings back to hold neck skin in place. Return legs to tucked position if untucked. Brush turkey with vegetable oil to prevent skin from drying. Insert meat thermometer into thickest part of thigh not touching bone.

Place unstuffed turkey, breast up, in center of rack over drip pan. Cover grill and leave vents open. Add 6 to 8 briquettes to each side every hour or as needed to maintain heat. Cook turkey to an internal thigh temperature of 180°F and breast to 170°F. A 4½- to 9-pound turkey will take about 1½ to 2½ hours.

To prepare corn and garlic for grilling, leave corn in husks and soak in cold water for 30 minutes. Carefully pull back husks and remove silks, leaving husks attached. Smooth husks over corn to enclose. Cut ½ inch off tip of garlic bulb; drizzle garlic with olive oil and wrap tightly in foil. Place corn and garlic on grill for last 30 to 40 minutes of grilling.

Remove husks and serve corn spread with melted butter and roasted garlic. *Serves 8*

● Preparation Time: 30 minutes plus grilling time ●

Nutritional Information per Serving (3 ounces cooked turkey):
Calories: 420, Fat: 15g, % of Calories from Fat: 33, Sodium: 135mg

*Grilled Turkey with
Roasted Garlic Grilled Corn*

Six O'Clock Sandwich

1 package (16 ounces) Butterball® Lean Turkey Smoked
    Sausage, cut into ½-inch diagonal slices
2 tablespoons olive oil
1 large onion, cut into lengthwise strips
1 yellow bell pepper, cut into thin strips
1 red bell pepper, cut into thin strips
1 can (14 ounces) artichoke hearts, drained and sliced thin
¼ cup fresh basil, shredded
1 loaf Italian bread, halved lengthwise
1½ cups (6 ounces) finely shredded Swiss cheese

Heat oil in large skillet over medium heat until hot. Cook and stir
onion and bell peppers until soft; add sausage. Cook and stir 10
minutes. Stir in artichokes and basil; remove from heat. Place
bread halves on baking sheet; top with half of cheese. Spoon
vegetable mixture over cheese; sprinkle with remaining cheese.
Place under broiler until cheese melts. Cut into 6 to 8 open-face
sandwiches.   *Makes 6 to 8 sandwiches*

● Preparation Time: 30 minutes ●

Nutritional Information per Serving *(8 servings):*
Calories: 400, Fat: 17g, % of Calories from Fat: 40, Sodium: 1040mg

TIP
*The Six O'Clock Sandwich is
also great to serve to a crowd. Make
several sandwiches ahead of time and
refrigerate until ready to
broil and serve.*

Six O'Clock Sandwich

Hidden Herb Grilled Turkey Breast

1 (3- to 9-pound) Butterball® Breast of Young Turkey, thawed
¼ cup coarsely chopped fresh parsley
2 tablespoons chopped mixed fresh herbs such as thyme,
  oregano and marjoram
2 tablespoons grated Parmesan cheese
1 teaspoon olive oil
½ teaspoon lemon juice
½ teaspoon salt
¼ teaspoon garlic powder
¼ teaspoon black pepper
  Vegetable oil

Prepare grill for indirect-heat grilling. Combine parsley, herbs,
Parmesan cheese, oil, lemon juice, salt, garlic powder and
pepper in medium bowl. Gently loosen and lift turkey skin from
surface of meat. Spread herb blend evenly over breast meat.
Replace skin over herb blend. Brush skin with vegetable oil.
Place turkey breast skin side up on prepared grill. Cover grill and
cook 1½ to 2½ hours for a 3- to 9-pound breast or until internal
temperature reaches 170°F and meat is no longer pink in center.
Number of servings varies

● Preparation Time: 15 minutes plus grilling time ●

Nutritional Information per Serving (3 ounces cooked turkey):
Calories: 180, Fat: 8g, % of Calories from Fat: 39, Sodium: 180mg

Crispy Parmesan-Peppercorn Pita Sandwiches

1 package (14 ounces) Butterball® Chicken Requests™
    Parmesan Crispy Baked Breasts
½ cup sprouts
¼ red onion, thin sliced, separated into rings
¼ cup prepared peppercorn ranch salad dressing
4 large pitas

Prepare chicken according to package directions. Cut one inch off top of each pita; open. Place chicken breasts, sprouts, onion and dressing in pitas. *Makes 4 sandwiches*

● Preparation Time: 20 minutes ●

Nutritional Information per Sandwich:
Calories: 440, Fat: 17g, % of Calories from Fat: 34, Sodium: 1000mg

Side by Side Southern Stuffing and Turkey

1 (3-pound) Butterball® Boneless Breast of Young Turkey with
    Gravy Packet, thawed
    Vegetable oil
1 can (14½ ounces) chicken broth
½ cup chopped onion
½ cup chopped celery
4 tablespoons butter or margarine
4 cups packaged cornbread stuffing
1 can (16 ounces) sliced peaches, drained and coarsely
    chopped
½ cup chopped pecans

Spray small roasting pan with nonstick cooking spray. Place boneless breast on one side of roasting pan. Brush with vegetable oil. Combine chicken broth, onion, celery and butter in large saucepan; simmer 5 minutes over low heat. Add stuffing, peaches and pecans; lightly toss mixture. Place stuffing alongside boneless breast. Cover stuffing with foil. Bake in preheated 325°F oven 1 hour and 45 minutes or until internal temperature reaches 170°F. Let boneless breast stand 10 minutes for easy carving. Prepare gravy according to package directions. Serve turkey with gravy and stuffing.   *Serves 6*

● Preparation Time: 15 minutes plus roasting time ●

Nutritional Information per Serving:
Calories: 390, Fat: 16g, % of Calories from Fat: 38, Sodium: 910mg

Crispy Baked Chicken Breasts with Italian-Herb Tortellini Salad

1 package (14 ounces) Butterball® Chicken Requests™ Italian Style Herb Crispy Baked Breasts
1 package (16 ounces) frozen cheese tortellini
1 cup chopped tomato
½ cup thin sliced cucumber
½ cup prepared Italian Parmesan salad dressing
3 tablespoons sliced ripe olives

Prepare chicken according to package directions. Cook and drain tortellini. Combine tortellini, tomato, cucumber, dressing and olives; toss to coat. Serve with chicken.   *Serves 4*

● Preparation Time: 20 minutes ●

Nutritional Information per Serving:
Calories: 690, Fat: 29g, % of Calories from Fat: 38, Sodium: 1340mg

Crispy Chicken Pub-Style Sandwiches

1 package (14 ounces) Butterball® Chicken Requests™ Lemon Pepper Crispy Baked Breasts
2 cups shredded cabbage
2 tablespoons malt vinegar
2 teaspoons sugar
2 teaspoons celery seed
2 tablespoons hearty-style mustard
8 slices pumpernickel bread

Prepare chicken according to package directions. Combine cabbage, vinegar, sugar and celery seed in small bowl. Spread mustard on four slices of bread; top each slice with chicken, malted cabbage and remaining bread slices.

Makes 4 sandwiches

● Preparation Time: 20 minutes ●

Nutritional Information per Sandwich:
Calories: 370, Fat: 8g, % of Calories from Fat: 19, Sodium: 850mg

Crispy Chicken Pizza Sandwiches

1 package (14 ounces) Butterball® Chicken Requests™ Italian Herb Crispy Baked Breasts
4 slices mozzarella cheese
4 Italian-style rolls, split
½ cup prepared pizza sauce
Red pepper flakes, optional

Prepare chicken according to package directions. Place slice of cheese on top of each chicken piece during the last minute of heating. Spread rolls with pizza sauce. Place chicken on rolls; sprinkle with red pepper flakes.

Makes 4 sandwiches

● Preparation Time: 20 minutes ●

Nutritional Information per Sandwich:
Calories: 420, Fat: 13g, % of Calories from Fat: 29, Sodium: 1160mg

Crispy Chicken Pub-Style Sandwich

Fashion and food from the 60's was fun then—and still is! Create diner favorites like classic Turkey á la King, hearty Bandstand Chili or piping hot Turkey Turnovers for a sure-fire taste extravaganza.

Bandstand Chili

2 cups chopped cooked Butterball® Boneless Young Turkey
1 tablespoon vegetable oil
1½ cups chopped onions
1½ cups chopped red bell pepper
2 tablespoons mild Mexican seasoning*
1 clove garlic, minced
1 can (28 ounces) tomato purée with tomato bits
1 can (15½ ounces) light red kidney beans, undrained

Heat oil in large skillet over medium heat until hot. Add onions, bell pepper, Mexican seasoning and garlic. Cook and stir 4 to 5 minutes. Add tomato purée and beans; stir in turkey. Reduce heat to low; simmer 5 minutes. *Serves 8*

*To make your own Mexican seasoning, combine 1 tablespoon chili powder, 1½ teaspoons oregano and 1½ teaspoons cumin.

● Preparation Time: 25 minutes ●

Nutritional Information per Serving:
Calories: 160, Fat: 4½g, % of Calories from Fat: 25, Sodium: 860mg

Low Fat Turkey Bacon Frittata

1 package (12 ounces) Butterball® Turkey Bacon, heated and chopped
6 ounces uncooked angel hair pasta, broken
2 teaspoons olive oil
1 small onion, sliced
1 red bell pepper, cut into thin strips
4 containers (4 ounces each) egg substitute
1 container (5 ounces) fat free ricotta cheese
1 cup (4 ounces) shredded fat free mozzarella cheese
1 cup (4 ounces) shredded reduced fat Swiss cheese
½ teaspoon salt
½ teaspoon black pepper
1 package (10 ounces) frozen spinach, thawed and squeezed dry

Cook and drain pasta. Heat oil in large skillet over medium heat until hot. Cook and stir onion and bell pepper until tender. Combine egg substitute, cheeses, salt, pepper and cooked pasta in large bowl. Add vegetables, spinach and turkey bacon. Spray 10-inch quiche dish with nonstick cooking spray; pour mixture into dish. Bake in preheated 350°F oven 30 minutes. Cut into wedges. Serve with spicy salsa, if desired.   *Serves 8*

● Preparation Time: 15 minutes plus baking time ●

Nutritional Information per Serving:
Calories: 280, Fat: 9g, % of Calories from Fat: 29, Sodium: 780mg

Low Fat Turkey Bacon Frittata

Creamy Wild Rice and Turkey Soup

2 cups chopped cooked Butterball® Breast of Young Turkey
1 tablespoon olive oil
1 cup finely chopped carrots
1 cup finely chopped onion
½ cup finely chopped celery
2 cloves garlic, minced
2 cans (14½ ounces each) chicken broth
2 cups cooked wild rice
½ cup whipping cream
  Salt and black pepper

Heat oil in large saucepan over medium heat until hot. Cook and stir carrots, onion, celery and garlic until onions are soft. Add chicken broth, wild rice and turkey; heat 10 minutes. Add whipping cream; cook over low heat until heated through. Add salt and pepper to taste.   *Makes 8 (1-cup) servings*

● Preparation Time: 30 minutes ●

Nutritional Information per Serving:
Calories: 180, Fat: 11g, % of Calories from Fat: 55, Sodium: 520mg

Turkey á la King

2 cups cubed Butterball® Fat Free Slice 'N Serve Oven
    Roasted Breast of Turkey, cubed
⅓ cup butter
4 ounces fresh mushrooms, sliced
4 tablespoons flour
½ teaspoon salt
⅛ teaspoon black pepper
1 can (14½ ounces) chicken broth
½ cup light cream
1 cup frozen peas and carrots
  Chopped fresh parsley

Melt butter in large saucepan over medium heat; add mushrooms. Cook and stir 5 minutes. Stir in flour, salt and pepper. Slowly blend in chicken broth and cream. Cook, stirring constantly, until thickened. Add turkey and peas and carrots. Heat well. Serve on toasted thick bread slices or pastry shells, if desired. Sprinkle with chopped parsley.   *Serves 4*

● Preparation Time: 25 minutes ●

Nutritional Information per Serving:
Calories: 320, Fat: 22g, % of Calories from Fat: 62, Sodium: 1190mg

Trim Turkey Tetrazzini

½ **pound Butterball® Oven Roasted Turkey Breast, sliced**
  ½ **inch thick in the deli, cubed**
½ **pound uncooked spaghetti, broken**
¼ **cup butter or margarine**
¼ **cup flour**
1 **can (14½ ounces) fat free reduced sodium chicken broth**
2¾ **cups milk**
½ **teaspoon salt**
¼ **teaspoon ground white pepper**
8 **ounces fresh mushrooms, sliced**
¼ **cup shredded Parmesan cheese**
½ **cup crumbled salad croutons**

Cook and drain spaghetti. Melt butter in large skillet over medium heat. Whisk in flour. Add chicken broth, milk, salt and pepper. Heat, stirring constantly, until thickened. Add turkey, mushrooms, Parmesan cheese and spaghetti to skillet. Spray 13×9-inch baking dish with nonstick cooking spray. Pour turkey mixture into baking dish. Top with crumbled croutons. Bake 30 to 40 minutes in preheated 350°F oven.   *Serves 8*

● Preparation Time: 15 minutes plus baking time ●

Nutritional Information per Serving:
Calories: 200, Fat: 8g, % of Calories from Fat: 35, Sodium: 700mg

Chicken Gone Garlic

1 Butterball® Fresh Young Roaster, giblets removed
3 tablespoons butter or margarine, softened
2 tablespoons minced fresh parsley
½ teaspoon poultry seasoning
½ teaspoon salt
¼ teaspoon cracked black pepper
   Juice of ½ lemon
4 heads garlic, cloves separated and peeled
4 large potatoes, cut into wedges
1 cup water

Combine butter, parsley, poultry seasoning, salt and pepper in small bowl. Pour lemon juice into cavity of chicken. Rub butter mixture on skin. Place chicken in roasting pan. Arrange garlic cloves and potatoes around chicken. Pour water into pan; cover. Roast 1 hour in preheated 375°F oven. Uncover and continue roasting 45 minutes to 1 hour or until internal temperature reaches 180°F in thigh and skin is golden brown.   *Serves 8*

● Preparation Time: 15 minutes plus roasting time ●

Nutritional Information per Serving:
Calories: 740, Fat: 49g, % of Calories from Fat: 59, Sodium: 660mg

TIP
To assure safe, tender, juicy poultry every time, use consistent doneness tests. For turkey and chicken, cook to an internal temperature of 180°–185°F in the deepest part of the thigh and 170°–175°F in the breast.

Chicken Gone Garlic

90's-Style Slow Cooker Coq Au Vin

**2 packages Butterball® Boneless Skinless Chicken Breast
  Fillets**
1 pound fresh mushrooms, sliced thick
1 jar (15 ounces) pearl onions, drained
½ cup dry white wine
1 teaspoon thyme leaves
1 bay leaf
1 cup chicken broth
⅓ cup flour
½ cup chopped fresh parsley

Place chicken, mushrooms, onions, wine, thyme and bay leaf
into slow cooker. Combine chicken broth and flour; pour into
slow cooker. Cover and cook 5 hours on low setting. Add
parsley. Serve over wild rice pilaf, if desired.   *Serves 8*

● Preparation Time: 30 minutes plus cooking time ●

Nutritional Information per Serving:
Calories: 180, Fat: 1g, % of Calories from Fat: 6, Sodium: 510mg

Turkey Turnovers

1 cup chopped cooked Butterball® Young Turkey
1 cup quartered fresh mushrooms
½ cup finely chopped onion
1 clove garlic, minced
1 tablespoon butter
  Dash dried thyme
1 tablespoon flour
⅓ cup whipping cream
3 tablespoons chopped fresh parsley
1 tablespoon chopped pimiento
¼ teaspoon salt
⅛ teaspoon black pepper
1 sheet frozen puff pastry, thawed
1 egg
1 tablespoon water

Cook and stir mushrooms, onion, garlic, butter and thyme in large skillet over medium heat until vegetables are soft. Add flour; cook, stirring constantly, until well blended. Stir in whipping cream. Cook, stirring constantly, until thickened. Add turkey, parsley, pimiento, salt and pepper; remove from heat. Roll pastry sheet into 10×12-inch square on lightly floured board. Cut into 4 rectangles. Spoon about one fourth turkey mixture onto center of each rectangle. Fold each rectangle into a triangle to cover filling. Moisten and press edges to seal in filling. Whisk egg with water; brush over top of pastry. Place on baking sheet. Bake in preheated 400°F oven 15 minutes.

Makes 4 turnovers

● Preparation Time: 30 minutes plus baking time ●

Nutritional Information per Turnover:
Calories: 360, Fat: 23g, % of Calories from Fat: 58, Sodium: 530mg

Rosemary Roasted Chicken and Potatoes

1 Butterball® Fresh Young Roaster, giblets removed
3 cloves garlic, minced
    Grated peel and juice of 1 lemon
2 tablespoons vegetable oil
1 tablespoon fresh rosemary leaves
1 teaspoon cracked black pepper
¼ teaspoon salt
6 medium potatoes, cut into pieces

Preheat oven to 425°F. Mix garlic, lemon peel, lemon juice, oil, rosemary, pepper and salt in medium bowl. Place chicken, breast side up, in lightly oiled large roasting pan. Place potatoes around chicken. Drizzle garlic mixture over chicken and onto potatoes. Bake 20 to 25 minutes per pound or until internal temperature reaches 180°F in thigh. Stir potatoes occasionally to brown evenly. Let chicken stand 10 minutes before carving.

Serves 8

● Preparation Time: 15 minutes plus roasting time ●

Nutritional Information per Serving:
Calories: 710, Fat: 48g, % of Calories from Fat: 61, Sodium: 540mg

Turkey Cutlets with Victory Garden Gravy

1 package Butterball® Fresh Boneless Turkey Breast Cutlets
½ cup milk
3 tablespoons flour
1 can(14½ ounces) chicken broth
2 cups broccoli florets
½ cup chopped plum tomatoes
1 tablespoon chopped fresh parsley
¼ teaspoon salt
¼ teaspoon black pepper
1 tablespoon vegetable oil
2 tablespoons grated Parmesan cheese

Whisk together milk and flour in small bowl. Combine milk mixture and chicken broth in large saucepan. Bring to a boil over medium-high heat, stirring constantly. Reduce heat to low; add broccoli. Simmer 5 minutes. Stir in tomatoes, parsley, salt and pepper. Heat oil in separate large skillet over medium heat until hot. Cook cutlets 2 to 2½ minutes on each side or until no longer pink in center. Serve with gravy. Sprinkle with Parmesan cheese. *Serves 4*

● Preparation Time: 15 minutes ●

Nutrition Information per Serving:
Calories: 197, Fat: 3½g, % of Calories from Fat: 14, Sodium: 730mg

Turkey Cutlets with
Victory Garden Gravy

Make It  & Take It

Choose from Turkey Calzones stuffed with oozing cheese, colorful Neon Turkey Pasta Salad or Muffaletta stacked high with luscious turkey, crisp lettuce and fresh tomatoes for the perfect packable treat.

Muffaletta

8 ounces Butterball® Honey Roasted and Smoked Turkey Breast, sliced thin in the deli
8 ounces Butterball® Oven Roasted Turkey Breast, sliced thin in the deli
1½ cups prepared fat free Italian salad dressing
⅓ cup salad olives
1 large loaf crusty round Italian bread
½ pound sliced Swiss cheese
½ pound sliced provolone cheese
Leaf lettuce
2 large tomatoes, sliced
1 red onion, sliced thin

Combine salad dressing and olives in small bowl. Slice bread in half crosswise. Spoon ½ cup dressing on bottom half of bread. Layer turkey, cheeses, lettuce, tomatoes and onion onto bread. Pour remaining dressing on top half of bread; place on top. Cut into 16 pieces to serve. *Serves 16*

● Preparation Time: 15 minutes ●

Nutritional Information per Serving:
Calories: 280, Fat: 7g, % of Calories from Fat: 25, Sodium: 1000mg

Neon Turkey Pasta Salad

2 cups cubed cooked Butterball® Breast of Young Turkey
2 cups tri-colored rotini pasta, cooked and drained
1 small zucchini, sliced
2 small tomatoes, cut into wedges
½ cup chunked yellow bell pepper
½ cup chunked red bell pepper
½ cup chunked green bell pepper
½ cup crumbled feta cheese
1 can (2¼ ounces) sliced ripe olives, drained
⅓ cup fresh basil leaves, cut into strips
1 cup prepared Italian salad dressing

Combine turkey, pasta, vegetables, cheese, olives and basil in large bowl. Toss with salad dressing. Chill at least 2 hours before serving. *Serves 6*

● Preparation Time: 20 minutes plus chilling time ●

Nutritional Information per Serving:
Calories: 620, Fat: 27g, % of Calories from Fat: 40, Sodium: 710mg

Pretzels with a Chicken Twist

2 packages Butterball® Chicken Breast Tenders, halved
**   lengthwise**
½ cup prepared honey mustard
2 cups crushed pretzels

Preheat oven to 400°F. Pour honey mustard into shallow bowl. Add chicken tenders and turn to coat. Discard any remaining honey mustard. Roll coated chicken in crushed pretzels. Place on baking sheet sprayed with nonstick cooking spray. Bake 5 to 8 minutes or until chicken is no longer pink in center. Serve with extra honey mustard for dipping. *Makes 32 appetizers*

● Preparation Time: 15 minutes ●

Nutritional Information per Serving (2 appetizers):
Calories: 70, Fat: 1g, % of Calories from Fat: 14, Sodium: 160mg

Neon Turkey Pasta Salad

Turkey Ranch Pasta Salad

2 cups cubed cooked Butterball® Boneless Breast of Turkey
4 cups penne pasta, cooked and drained
1 cup sliced (¼ inch thick) and halved zucchini
1 cup sliced (¼ inch thick) and halved yellow squash
½ cup sliced green onions
½ cup red bell pepper strips
½ cup green bell pepper strips
1 cup prepared ranch salad dressing
½ cup finely shredded Parmesan cheese
  Salt and black pepper

Combine turkey, pasta, zucchini, squash, onions and bell peppers in large bowl. Toss with salad dressing and Parmesan cheese. Add salt and pepper to taste. Chill.   *Serves 8*

● Preparation Time: 25 minutes plus chilling time ●

Nutritional Information per Serving:
Calories: 360, Fat: 19g, % of Calories from Fat: 47, Sodium: 490mg

Turkey Calzones

1 package (1¼ pounds) Butterball® Lean Fresh Ground Turkey
1 cup prepared pizza sauce
2 tablespoons chopped fresh parsley
2 tubes (12 ounces each) refrigerated large biscuits (10 per tube)
¾ cup low fat ricotta cheese
1¼ cups (5 ounces) shredded low fat mozzarella cheese
1 egg white
1 tablespoon water
  Grated Parmesan cheese

Cook ground turkey according to package directions for crumbles. Remove from heat. Stir in pizza sauce and parsley. Place biscuits on lightly floured surface; flatten each into 3- to 4-inch circle. Place dollop of turkey mixture, ricotta and mozzarella cheese on half of each circle. Lightly moisten edges with water; fold circles in half. Gently press to seal and enclose filling. Combine egg white and water. Place filled calzones on baking sheet. Brush with egg white mixture; sprinkle with Parmesan cheese. Bake in preheated 400°F oven 10 to 15 minutes or until golden brown. Serve with additional pizza sauce.

Makes 20 calzones

● Preparation Time: 30 minutes ●

Note: These can be baked and reheated later in preheated 400°F oven 6 to 8 minutes.

Nutritional Information per Calzone:
Calories: 190, Fat: 10g, % of Calories from Fat: 47, Sodium: 520mg

I Have to Bring Something!! Turkey Roll-Ups

1 package (6 ounces) Butterball® Fat Free Oven Roasted Deli-Thin Sliced Turkey Breast
1 container (8 ounces) soft cream cheese
½ cup prepared medium-hot salsa
2 green onions, chopped
2 tablespoons minced fresh cilantro
6 (10-inch) flour tortillas
1 red bell pepper, cut into strips
2 cups shredded lettuce

Combine cream cheese, salsa, onions and cilantro in medium bowl. Spread cream cheese mixture on tortillas; top with turkey slices. Place bell pepper and lettuce on turkey. Roll tortillas into pinwheels. Cut each pinwheel into fourths.

Makes 24 appetizers

● Preparation Time: 15 minutes ●

Nutritional Information per Appetizer:
Calories: 68, Fat: 3g, % of Calories from Fat: 44, Sodium: 173mg

Little Turkey Travelers

2 pounds Butterball® Peppered Turkey Breast, sliced thin in the deli
1 jar (16 ounces) mild pepper rings, drained
1 can (14 ounces) artichoke hearts, drained and quartered
1 jar (8 ounces) mild giardiniera, undrained
1 jar (7 ounces) roasted red peppers, drained and cut into wide strips
2 packages (8 ounces each) soft cream cheese with chives and onion
1 package (17 ounces) soft cracker bread (three 16-inch round flat breads)
½ pound thinly sliced provolone cheese

Combine mild peppers, artichoke hearts, giardiniera and roasted peppers in medium bowl. Spread cream cheese on each flat bread. Place turkey and cheese slices on each bread; top each with 1½ cups vegetable mixture.* Roll tightly, jelly-roll style, beginning at the filled end. Wrap each roll in plastic wrap. Chill 2 hours. Cut each roll into 16 slices.   *Makes 48 appetizers*

*For better roll sealing, leave 4 inches across top of each bread covered with cream cheese only.

● Preparation Time: 30 minutes plus chilling time ●

Nutritional Information per Serving (2 appetizers):
Calories: 240, Fat: 14g, % of Calories from Fat: 50, Sodium: 750mg

COOKING FOR A CROWD

Impress party guests with spicy Turkey Sausage Jambalaya or mouthwatering Buffet Cranberry Biscuits with Smoked Turkey. With these and many more crowd-pleasing recipes, all your gatherings are sure to be a smash.

The Long or The Short of It

2 pounds Butterball® Oven Roasted Turkey Breast, sliced in the deli

2 pounds Butterball® Honey Roasted and Smoked Turkey Breast, sliced in the deli

2 (3-foot) loaves submarine sandwich bread *or* 32 mini kaiser rolls

3 cups mayonnaise

1 jar (8 ounces) country Dijon mustard

2 pounds dill cheese, sliced

1 pound cojack cheese, sliced

2 large red bell peppers, sliced

2 large green bell peppers, sliced

4 large ripe tomatoes, sliced

1 large Spanish onion, sliced

1 head lettuce, shredded

Cut bread or rolls in half horizontally. Spread with mayonnaise and mustard. Layer turkey, cheeses, bell peppers, tomatoes, onion and lettuce on bottom half of bread. Close sandwich. Cut each submarine loaf into 16 sandwiches. *Serves 32*

● Preparation Time: 30 minutes ●

Nutritional Information per Serving:
Calories: 640, Fat: 34g, % of Calories from Fat: 47, Sodium: 1440mg

Rotisserie Chicken with Pesto Brush

2 Butterball® Fresh Young Roasters
¼ cup chopped fresh oregano
¼ cup chopped fresh parsley
2 tablespoons chopped fresh rosemary
2 tablespoons chopped fresh thyme
½ cup olive oil
½ cup balsamic vinegar

Combine oregano, parsley, rosemary, thyme, oil and vinegar in small bowl. Roast chicken according to rotisserie directions. Dip brush into herb mixture; brush chicken with herb mixture every 30 minutes for first 2 hours of roasting. Brush every 15 minutes during last hour of roasting. Roast chicken until internal temperature reaches 180°F in thigh and meat is no longer pink.

Serves 16

● Preparation Time: 15 minutes plus roasting time ●

Nutritional Information per Serving:
Calories: 280, Fat: 23g, % of Calories from Fat: 71, Sodium: 170mg

TIP
To make an aromatic herb brush,
bundle sprigs of rosemary, thyme, oregano
and parsley together. Tie bundle with kitchen
string. Use as brush for pesto.

Rotisserie Chicken with Pesto Brush

Grilled Lemon Minted Chicken Breasts

3 packages Butterball® Chicken Split Breasts
1 cup fresh lemon juice
¼ cup chopped fresh mint leaves
2 teaspoons grated lemon peel
½ teaspoon red pepper flakes

Combine lemon juice, mint leaves, lemon peel and red pepper flakes in small bowl. Grill chicken, bone side up, over hot coals 15 to 20 minutes, brushing frequently with lemon mixture. Turn and grill chicken 15 to 20 minutes longer or until internal temperature reaches 170°F and no longer pink in center. Serve grilled chicken with lemon minted couscous.*   *Serves 9*

*To prepare lemon minted couscous, prepare couscous according to package directions. Add a squeeze of fresh lemon and chopped fresh mint.

● Preparation Time: 30 to 40 minutes ●

Nutritional Information per Serving:
Calories: 140, Fat: 1½g, % of Calories from Fat: 10, Sodium: 80mg

Backyard Barbecue Turkey Burgers

2 packages (1¼ pounds each) Butterball® Lean Fresh Ground Turkey
1 cup chopped onion
1 cup prepared barbecue sauce*, divided
1 cup dry bread crumbs
1 teaspoon salt
¼ teaspoon black pepper
12 hamburger buns, toasted

Combine ground turkey, onion, ½ cup barbecue sauce, bread crumbs, salt and pepper in large bowl. Mix until thoroughly combined. Form into 12 patties. Grill over hot coals 5 to 6 minutes on each side or cook in large nonstick skillet over medium heat 10 to 12 minutes or until no longer pink in center. Turn 2 to 3 times for even browning. Serve on buns with remaining ½ cup barbecue sauce on the side.

Makes 12 burgers

*Tastes best with a sweet and smoky barbecue sauce.

● Preparation Time: 15 minutes ●

Nutritional Information per Burger:
Calories: 300, Fat: 10g, % of Calories from Fat: 30, Sodium: 690mg

Turkey Sausage Jambalaya

2 packages Butterball® Lean Fresh Turkey Hot Italian Sausage
2 tablespoons vegetable oil
2 cups chopped onion
⅔ cup chopped green bell pepper
⅔ cup chopped red bell pepper
⅔ cup chopped celery
4 to 6 cloves garlic, minced
4 cups chopped tomato
¼ to ½ teaspoon cayenne pepper
¼ teaspoon ground thyme
2 cans (14½ ounces each) chicken broth
2 cups uncooked long grain rice
⅓ cup chopped fresh parsley
Salt and black pepper

Heat oil in large skillet over medium heat until hot. Brown turkey sausage in skillet 8 minutes, turning occasionally. Add onion, bell peppers, celery and garlic. Cook and stir 3 to 5 minutes. Stir in tomato, cayenne pepper and thyme. Add chicken broth; bring to a boil. Stir in rice; cover. Reduce heat to low; simmer 20 minutes. Remove from heat. Stir in parsley. Add salt and pepper to taste. Cover; let stand 5 minutes before serving.

Serves 10

● Preparation Time: 30 to 40 minutes ●

Nutritional Information per Serving:
Calories: 350, Fat: 13g, % of Calories from Fat: 31, Sodium: 930mg

Buffet Cranberry Biscuits with Smoked Turkey

1 Butterball® Fully Cooked Smoked Young Turkey, thawed, sliced thin
3½ cups packaged biscuit mix
2 tablespoons butter or margarine
¾ cup dried cranberries
1 cup milk

Cranberry Butter:
½ cup butter
¼ cup honey
¼ cup dried cranberries

Place biscuit mix in large bowl. Cut in butter with pastry blender until mixture resembles coarse crumbs. Stir in cranberries; add milk. Stir until soft dough forms. Turn dough onto lightly floured surface; knead gently 10 times. Roll to ½-inch thickness. Cut 20 biscuits with 2½-inch round cutter. Place on ungreased baking sheet. Bake in preheated 400°F oven 10 minutes or until golden brown.

To prepare Cranberry Butter, combine butter, honey and cranberries in food processor; process just until blended.

To assemble sandwiches, split each biscuit in half. Spread each biscuit half generously with cranberry butter. Stack turkey on bottom of each biscuit. Place top half of biscuit on turkey.

Makes 20 buffet sandwiches

● Preparation Time: 30 minutes ●

Note: Biscuits and butter can be made a few hours prior to serving.

Nutritional Information per Buffet Sandwich:
Calories: 230, Fat: 12g, % of Calories from Fat: 48, Sodium: 430mg

Buffet Cranberry Biscuits with Smoked Turkey

California Thin Crust Pizza with Smoked Turkey

1 Butterball® Fully Cooked Smoked Young Turkey, thawed, sliced thin
½ cup mayonnaise
3 tablespoons grated Parmesan cheese
1 tube (10 ounces) prepared pizza dough
1 teaspoon dried oregano, divided
¼ cup sun-dried tomato bits, packed in oil
1 can (14 ounces) artichoke hearts, drained and chopped
1 cup crumbled feta cheese

Combine mayonnaise and Parmesan cheese in small bowl; set aside. Spray 15×10-inch jelly-roll pan with nonstick cooking spray. Press dough into pan. Sprinkle dough with ½ teaspoon oregano. Bake in preheated 425°F oven 8 to 10 minutes or until crust begins to brown. Remove from oven; spread with mayonnaise mixture. Sprinkle turkey, tomato bits, artichoke hearts and feta cheese on top of crust. Top with remaining ½ teaspoon oregano. Bake 10 to 12 minutes longer until crust is browned and toppings are heated through.

Makes 24 appetizers

● Preparation Time: 30 minutes ●

Nutritional Information per Appetizer:
Calories: 100, Fat: 5g, % of Calories from Fat: 45, Sodium: 310mg

California Thin Crust Pizza with Smoked Turkey

Product Index

Chicken Breasts
Grilled Lemon Minted
Chicken Breasts, 86
Jalapeño Grilled Chicken
with Baja Pasta, 25

Chicken Breasts, Boneless
Ranch-Style Chicken and
Pasta, 38

Chicken Fillets
Chicken Marsala, 33
Chicken Seville, 50
Grilled Chicken Breasts with
Tropical Salsa, 26
Louisiana Zydeco Chicken,
28
90's-Style Slow Cooker Coq
Au Vin, 70

Chicken Requests™
Antipasto Dinner Salad,
10
Crispy Baked Chicken
Breasts with Italian-Herb
Tortellini Salad, 59
Crispy Chicken Pizza
Sandwiches, 60
Crispy Chicken Pub-Style
Sandwiches, 60
Crispy Chicken with
Mushroom Fusilli Pasta,
43
Crispy Italian Herb Chicken
with Tri-Color Rotini Pasta,
34
Crispy Lemon Pepper
Chicken with Spinach
Pasta, 36
Crispy Parmesan Chicken
with Penne Pasta
Primavera, 44

Crispy Parmesan-
Peppercorn Pita
Sandwiches, 58
Crispy Southwestern
Seasoned Chicken with
Pasta Fideo, 38
Oriental Dinner Salad, 10

Chicken Tenders
Chicken Caesar Salad, 8
Pretzels with a Chicken
Twist, 76
Thai Stir Fry, 20

Chicken, Boneless Thighs
Quickest Chicken Cacciatore,
16

Chicken, Whole
Chicken Gone Garlic, 68
Rosemary Roasted Chicken
and Potatoes, 71
Rotisserie Chicken with
Pesto Brush, 84

Turkey Bacon
Low Fat Turkey Bacon
Frittata, 64

Turkey Breast
Creamy Wild Rice and
Turkey Soup, 66
Hidden Herb Grilled Turkey
Breast, 56
Neon Turkey Pasta Salad, 76

Turkey Breast, Boneless
Side by Side Southern
Stuffing and Turkey, 58
Turkey Ranch Pasta Salad, 78
Turkey with Fiery Thai
Sauce, 26

Turkey Breast, Slice 'N Serve
  Pesto Pasta Turkey Toss,
    39
  Turkey á la King, 66

Turkey Cutlets
  Moroccan Grilled Turkey
    with Cucumber Yogurt
    Sauce, 30
  Nutty-Crusted Turkey
    Cutlets, 40
  Turkey Cutlets with Chipotle
    Pepper Mole, 22
  Turkey Cutlets with Tex-Mex
    Salsa, 50
  Turkey Cutlets with Victory
    Garden Gravy, 72

Turkey Italian Sausage
  Butterball® Sweet Italian
    Sausage with Vesuvio
    Potatoes, 11
  Chicago Fire Italian Sausage
    Sandwiches, 48
  Turkey Sausage Jambalaya,
    87

Turkey Medallions
  South of the Border Turkey
    Kabobs, 46

Turkey Smoked Sausage
  Hearty Turkey Soup, 28
  Six O'Clock Sandwich, 54

Turkey Strips
  Matchstick Stir Fry, 24
  Turkey Tostadas, 14

Turkey Tenderloins
  Caribbean Grilled Turkey,
    32
  Mustard Herb Crusted
    Turkey Tenderloins, 51
  Turkey Tenderloin with
    Mushroom Sauce, 42

Turkey, Boneless
  Bandstand Chili, 62
  Turkey with Hoisin Sauce and
    Oriental Vegetables, 29

Turkey, Deli
  "Let's Talk Turkey" From The
    Deli, 18
  Little Turkey Travelers, 80
  Long or The Short of It, The,
    82
  Muffaletta, 74
  Pasta and Spinach with Sun-
    Dried Tomatoes, 42
  Trim Turkey Tetrazzini, 67

Turkey, Ground
  Backyard Barbecue Turkey
    Burgers, 86
  Grilled Jalapeño Turkey
    Burgers, 6
  Turkey Calzones, 78
  Turkey Stuffed Chiles
    Rellenos, 32
  Turkey Tortilla Soup, 17

Turkey, Packaged Deli Slices
  I Have to Bring Something!!
    Turkey Roll-Ups, 79
  Turkey on Focaccia Rolls, 12

**Turkey, Smoked, Fully
  Cooked**
  Buffet Cranberry Biscuits
    with Smoked Turkey, 88
  California Thin Crust Pizza
    with Smoked Turkey, 90
  Smoked Turkey with
    Summer Cranberry Nectar,
    48
  Turkey Apple Grill, 16

Turkey, Whole
  Grilled Turkey with Roasted
    Garlic Grilled Corn, 52
  Turkey Turnovers, 70

Recipe Index

Antipasto Dinner Salad, 10

Backyard Barbecue Turkey Burgers, 86
Baja Pasta, 25
Bandstand Chili, 62
Buffet Cranberry Biscuits with Smoked Turkey, 88
Butterball® Sweet Italian Sausage with Vesuvio Potatoes, 11

California Thin Crust Pizza with Smoked Turkey, 90
Caribbean Grilled Turkey, 32
Chicago Fire Italian Sausage Sandwiches, 48
Chicken Caesar Salad, 8
Chicken Gone Garlic, 68
Chicken Marsala, 33
Chicken Seville, 50
Creamy Wild Rice and Turkey Soup, 66
Crispy Baked Chicken Breasts with Italian-Herb Tortellini Salad, 59
Crispy Chicken Pizza Sandwiches, 60
Crispy Chicken Pub-Style Sandwiches, 60
Crispy Chicken with Mushroom Fusilli Pasta, 43
Crispy Italian Herb Chicken with Tri-Color Rotini Pasta, 34
Crispy Lemon Pepper Chicken with Spinach Pasta, 36
Crispy Parmesan Chicken with Penne Pasta Primavera, 44
Crispy Parmesan-Peppercorn Pita Sandwiches, 58
Crispy Southwestern Seasoned Chicken with Pasta Fideo, 38
Cucumber Yogurt Sauce, 30

Grilled Chicken Breasts with Tropical Salsa, 26
Grilled Jalapeño Turkey Burgers, 6
Grilled Lemon Minted Chicken Breasts, 86
Grilled Turkey with Roasted Garlic Grilled Corn, 52

Hearty Turkey Soup, 28
Hidden Herb Grilled Turkey Breast, 56

I Have to Bring Something!! Turkey Roll-Ups, 79

Jalapeño Grilled Chicken with Baja Pasta, 25

"Let's Talk Turkey" From The Deli, 18
Little Turkey Travelers, 80
Long or The Short of It, The, 82
Louisiana Zydeco Chicken, 28
Low Fat Turkey Bacon Frittata, 64

Matchstick Stir Fry, 24
Moroccan Grilled Turkey with Cucumber Yogurt Sauce, 30
Muffaletta, 74
Mustard Herb Crusted Turkey Tenderloins, 51

Neon Turkey Pasta Salad, 76
90's-Style Slow Cooker Coq Au Vin, 70
Nutty-Crusted Turkey Cutlets, 40

Oriental Dinner Salad, 10

Pasta and Spinach with Sun-Dried Tomatoes, 42
Pesto Pasta Turkey Toss, 39
Pretzels with a Chicken Twist, 76

Quickest Chicken Cacciatore, 16

Ranch-Style Chicken and Pasta, 38
Rosemary Roasted Chicken and Potatoes, 71
Rotisserie Chicken with Pesto Brush, 84

Side by Side Southern Stuffing and Turkey, 58
Six O'Clock Sandwich, 54
Smoked Turkey with Summer Cranberry Nectar, 48
South of the Border Turkey Kabobs, 46

Thai Stir Fry, 20
Trim Turkey Tetrazzini, 67
Turkey á la King, 66
Turkey Apple Grill, 16
Turkey Calzones, 78
Turkey Cutlets with Chipotle Pepper Mole, 22
Turkey Cutlets with Tex-Mex Salsa, 50
Turkey Cutlets with Victory Garden Gravy, 72
Turkey on Focaccia Rolls, 12
Turkey Ranch Pasta Salad, 78
Turkey Sausage Jambalaya, 87
Turkey Stuffed Chiles Rellenos, 32
Turkey Tenderloin with Mushroom Sauce, 42
Turkey Tortilla Soup, 17
Turkey Tostadas, 14
Turkey Turnovers, 70
Turkey with Fiery Thai Sauce, 26
Turkey with Hoisin Sauce and Oriental Vegetables, 29

Notes

METRIC CONVERSION CHART

VOLUME MEASUREMENTS (dry)

⅛ teaspoon = 0.5 mL

¼ teaspoon = 1 mL

½ teaspoon = 2 mL

¾ teaspoon = 4 mL

1 teaspoon = 5 mL

1 tablespoon = 15 mL

2 tablespoons = 30 mL

¼ cup = 60 mL

⅓ cup = 75 mL

½ cup = 125 mL

⅔ cup = 150 mL

¾ cup = 175 mL

1 cup = 250 mL

2 cups = 1 pint = 500 mL

3 cups = 750 mL

4 cups = 1 quart = 1 L

VOLUME MEASUREMENTS (fluid)

1 fluid ounce (2 tablespoons) = 30 mL

4 fluid ounces (½ cup) = 125 mL

8 fluid ounces (1 cup) = 250 mL

12 fluid ounces (1½ cups) = 375 mL

16 fluid ounces (2 cups) = 500 mL

WEIGHTS (mass)

½ ounce = 15 g

1 ounce = 30 g

3 ounces = 90 g

4 ounces = 120 g

8 ounces = 225 g

10 ounces = 285 g

12 ounces = 360 g

16 ounces = 1 pound = 450 g

DIMENSIONS

1/16 inch = 2 mm

⅛ inch = 3 mm

¼ inch = 6 mm

½ inch = 1.5 cm

¾ inch = 2 cm

1 inch = 2.5 cm

OVEN TEMPERATURES

250°F = 120°C

275°F = 140°C

300°F = 150°C

325°F = 160°C

350°F = 180°C

375°F = 190°C

400°F = 200°C

425°F = 220°C

450°F = 230°C

BAKING PAN SIZES

Utensil	Size in Inches/ Quarts	Metric Volume	Size in Centimeters
Baking or Cake Pan (square or rectangular)	8×8×2	2 L	20×20×5
	9×9×2	2.5 L	23×23×5
	12×8×2	3 L	30×20×5
	13×9×2	3.5 L	33×23×5
Loaf Pan	8×4×3	1.5 L	20×10×7
	9×5×3	2 L	23×13×7
Round Layer Cake Pan	8×1½	1.2 L	20×4
	9×1½	1.5 L	23×4
Pie Plate	8×1¼	750 mL	20×3
	9×1¼	1 L	23×3
Baking Dish or Casserole	1 quart	1 L	—
	1½ quart	1.5 L	—
	2 quart	2 L	—